Published by

James H. Kaster

Concord, NC

Printed in the United States of America

ISBN: 978-0-982-82208-1

The information contained within this book is true and complete to the best of my knowledge. Material was gathered from manufacturers' brochures, advertisements and media kits. Information is provided without any guarantee on the part of the publisher. Publisher also disclaims any liability incurred from use of this information.

© 2010 by James H. Kaster

All rights reserved. No part of this publication may be reproduced or transmitted in any form or by any means, electronic or mechanical, including photocopy, scanning, recording or any information retrieval system without permission in writing from the publisher. Permission is never granted for commercial purposes.

Manufacturer, vehicle, model, trim names and/or designations are the trademarks of their respective companies. They are used for identification purposes only. This is not an official publication of any of these companies or manufacturers.

Table of Contents

Table of Contents	2
Opera Windows	3
AMC	4
Buick	5
Cadillac	8
Chevrolet	10
Chrysler	12
Dodge	14
Ford	16
Lincoln	19
Mercury	21
Oldsmobile	23
Plymouth	26
Pontiac	27
Opera Lamps	29
Index	34

1978 Chrysler Cordoba

Opera Windows

With each passing generation, attention in collectible cars migrates to vehicles of more recent decades. Perhaps this is the result of younger enthusiasts, remembering their childhood cars, entering the hobby for the first time. Perhaps it's the low entry price of acquiring a classic from later models. Maybe it takes time to appreciate the designs and styles of a recent, past generation. Whatever the reason, cars of the 1970s and 1980s are now entering classic and collectible status and one American automotive design trend that is ubiquitous throughout those decades is the opera window.

Opera windows invoked an image of passengers being chauffeured in secluded privacy, to a stately night on the town, while wearing one's finest attire. These small windows enabled rear seat passengers to peer out on the town, landscape and scenery while outsiders looked in with mysterious wonderment about who may be inside such a fine automobile.

Sometimes called a coach window or landau roof, we know what an opera window is when we see it. Yet, it can be difficult to define as the styling language differed from manufacturer, model and year. The Random House definition is "a narrow, fixed window on each side of the rear passenger compartment of an automobile." That's a good start. But, I think there's more to it than just a physical description. I believe there are intrinsic, emotive values that add to the mystique of an opera window. For example, while Random House defines the window as being narrow, that's a relative term. A better qualifier would suggest a feeling of privacy that a rear seat passenger may experience while riding inside the car. I, hereby, define an opera window as having the following characteristics:

- Fixed side window located in the B or C pillar
- Styled so that the opera window does not appear to be an extension of the door windows
- Promotes fashion over function
  - <u>Glass Décor</u>: May be embellished with stripes, scripts, badges, beveling, etc.
  - <u>Trim</u>: May include roof trim, such as crown or tiara-band moldings, vinyl top, padding, opera lamps, etc.
- Conjures a feeling of privacy and mystery for the rear seat passengers. The following create a more intimate experience:
  - <u>Glass</u>: Smaller windows and reducing the number of window panes in the rear seat to 1
  - <u>Ratio</u>: Window size related to the rear quarter, disrupting a single, large greenhouse look
  - <u>Doors</u>: 2-door cars are inherently more private due to the lack of a rear door with its window. However, 4-door cars actually gained rear/side visibility advantages from an opera window being added to the C-pillar where they had not existed before.

By my definition, some pre-war vehicles may appear to have opera windows, such as the 1925 Stearns-Knight (shown left) and the 1925-26 Buick Master Six Coupes/Broughams, to name a couple. Some suggest that the first and last generation Thunderbird as the bookends of the opera window trend with their round port holes. However, since these cars were two-seaters, they don't meet my requirement of an opera window catering to rear seat passengers. To me, they remain as port holes that added equally to the function of visibility as it did to making a fashion statement.

As a universal design trend and language, it was in the 1970s and 1980s when this style flourished among US auto manufacturers; with a few stragglers in the 90s holding on to their aging demographic target. This book, therefore, focuses on America cars from this era. Yet, I show cars where you (and I) may question the accuracy of their inclusion as having an opera window. Does surrounding fixed glass with vinyl qualify it as an opera window when the window size is large in proportion to the roofline/greenhouse? Some say yes. I leave it to my readers to decide.

If the Thunderbirds aren't the true bookends of the opera window trend, what are? While many believe the 1972 Continental Mark IV's oval opera window as the most recognizable start, I believe the 1971 Cadillac Eldorado should get the credit as the first mass production opera window. Lincoln deserves the kudos for popularizing the trend and staying longest at the party with their 1997 Town Car.

1971 Cadillac Eldorado   1997 Lincoln Town Car

James H. Kaster

AMC

1981 AMC Concord coupe and sedan

1976 AMC Hornet (example of a Concord without an opera window)

1978 & 1979 AMC Concord sported an almost triangular opera window within its vinyl roof.

1980-1983 AMC Concord & Eagle sedan

1980-1983 AMC Concord & Eagle coupe

1976 AMC Matador with Barcelona package and luxury roof.

1976 AMC Matador (base roof without opera window)

American Automotive Design Trends: Opera Windows – Fashion over Function

BUICK

1976 Buick Electra Limited Park Avenue

1974 Buick LeSabre – Does it or doesn't it have an opera window? This is debated by many due to the large size of the glass and overall open greenhouse with little privacy.

1975 Buick Electra – Coupe in foreground (with a halo-vinyl roof treatment) and sedan in background, both, reveal their opera windows.

1978 Buick Electra

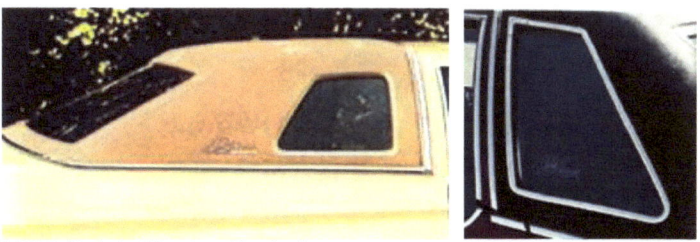
1976 Buick Electra Park Avenue coupe (left) with a smaller opera window than the 1975 Electra. 1975 Buick Electra Park Avenue sedan (right).

1985 Buick LeSabre – Another debatable example. Is it or isn't it an opera window?

1981 Buick Electra coupe. The '81, though well trimmed, like the '85 LeSabre at left, may or may not be an opera window to some. The large glass area, coupled with a vinyl roof and trim around three of the four sides, challenges onlookers to define it as an opera window.

American Automotive Design Trends: Opera Windows – Fashion over Function

1973 Buick Century 350 Colonnade. The coupe above exemplifies a substantial fixed window that seems to be a design element intended to be more functional as part of a large greenhouse.

1973 Buick Century Regal Colonnade – with some vinyl and trim, a large glass area becomes narrow and private. In the early 70s, full vinyl roofs, like this, were desirable.

1984 Buick Century – The half-vinyl roof and over-the-roof chrome molding do little to convince anyone that this could be an opera window.

1981 Buick Regal Limited – Most opera window fashion elements are visible here: half-vinyl roof, crown molding, opera window and badges.

1978 Buick Regal – Close to true opera window classification, this small window is well trimmed, but not as nicely bordered as windows completely dressed in vinyl. Without the trim the window looks like a continuous extension of the driver's door window.

1976 Buick Skylark – The half-vinyl roof hides a larger rear side glass window on other Skylark trim levels. Yet, Buick manages to craft a more functional opera window due to this window's medium size.

1985 Buick Somerset Regal – This new model, renamed simply as Somerset in future years, displays GM's move away from opera windows and embrace large glass for better rear/side visibility.

1974 Buick Riviera – Full-vinyl roof (top), undressed roof (above left), and view from inside (above right).

1976 Buick Riviera – Shown with "thickly-padded landau top and roof crown molding" option.

1975 Buick Riviera

1978 Buick Riviera – The 1977 & 1978 Riviera got a new chassis, body, interior and a smaller opera window with an angled bottom line.

CADILLAC

Styling. It's all-new and all-Cadillac, a carefully created combination of styling continuity and contemporary flair. The classic Cadillac look is accented by such styling innovations as the jewel-like stand-up crest of the Eldorado, the new coach windows in the Eldorado Coupe and the sleek, new roof line of the Brougham.

1971 Cadillac Eldorado – Initially, Cadillac called them "coach windows". The Eldorado was the first to market with this styling trend that would soon, thereafter, be available in cars of all size and price ranges.

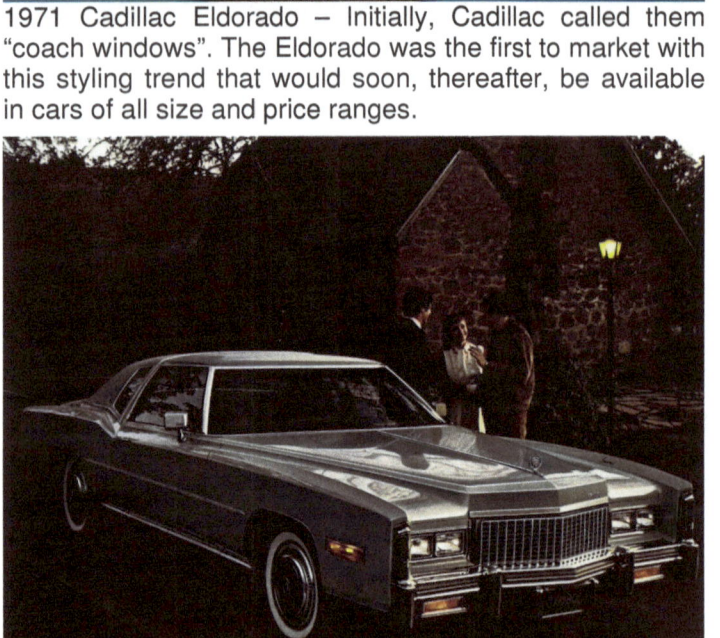

1976 Cadillac Eldorado

1974 Cadillac Eldorado – While the opera window maintained its same shape as 1971, the vinyl roof's beltline gains a curve with the Custom Cabriolet option.

1975 Cadillac Eldorado – Showing more evolutionary angles on the window's and vinyl roof's beltline.

1977 Cadillac Eldorado Biarritz

American Automotive Design Trends: Opera Windows – Fashion over Function

1975 Cadillac Sedan deVille

1974 Cadillac Calais coupe and sedan – Note how the 1975 Sedan deVille (above) added a C-pillar opera window, compared to 1974, which aids the driver's rear/side vision.

1974 Cadillac Coupe deVille – d'Elegance with Cabriolet roof (top) and full-padded vinyl roof (below)

1987 Cadillac Coupe deVille

1977 Cadillac Coupe deVille with Cabriolet vinyl roof

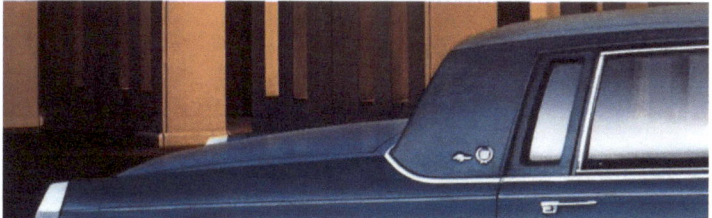
1988 Cadillac Brougham d'Elegance – A popular trick used by GM and Chrysler was adding vinyl and trim to the rear door's quarter window to construct that opera window feel.

1988 Cadillac Brougham – without d'Elegance trim and standard rear quarter door window.

1981 Cadillac Fleetwood Brougham Coupe – Fully dressed with a padded-vinyl roof, badges, chrome moldings and electro-luminescent opera lamps.

American Automotive Design Trends: Opera Windows – Fashion over Function

CHEVROLET

1975 Chevrolet Caprice Classic Sport Sedan – Brochure refers to the C-pillar windows as simply "rear quarter windows"

1974 Chevrolet Caprice Classic Coupe – Is this glass area too large to be called an opera window?

1975 Chevrolet Caprice Classic Sport Sedan – Note the opera window above the rear seat back.

1975 Chevrolet Impala Sport Sedan

1975 Chevrolet Impala Custom

1987 Chevrolet Caprice Classic Brougham

1987 Chevrolet Caprice LS Brougham – Adds a half-vinyl roof and rear door quarter opera window to the standard Caprice line (shown at left).

1974 Chevrolet Chevelle – A sibling in GM's family of Colonnade styled cars with the large rear side window.

1974 Chevrolet Chevelle Laguna Type S-3 Colonnade Hardtop Coupe (top) and Malibu Classic Coupe (above)

1973 Chevrolet Monte Carlo

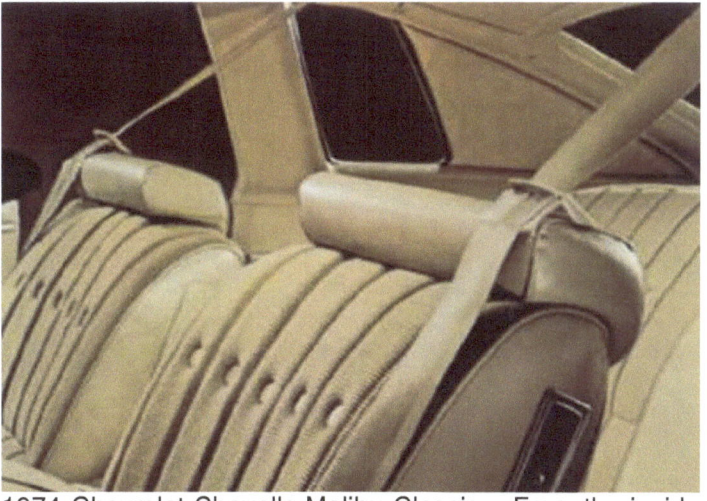

1974 Chevrolet Chevelle Malibu Classic – From the inside – Note the interior window trim that reduces the size of the large window (top left) to a narrow opera window.

1981 Chevrolet Monte Carlo – Chevy skips the opera window look from 1978 to 1980 and brings them back in 1981.

1976 Chevrolet Monza Towne Coupe

1976 Chevrolet Concours Coupe with Cabriolet vinyl roof

1981 Chevrolet Malibu Classic Landau Coupe – Trying to maintain the opera fashion without the narrow window, Chevy adds a half-vinyl roof and special B-pillar molding.

American Automotive Design Trends: Opera Windows – Fashion over Function

CHRYSLER

1975 Chrysler Cordoba with Landau roof – *"the new small Chrysler"*

1978 Chrysler Cordoba with optional Crown roof and special "over-the-top" illuminated light band.

1980 Chrysler Cordoba Corinthian Edition

1975 Chrysler Cordoba – Inside looking out – Note courtesy lamp mounted below the opera window.

1978 Chrysler LeBaron Medallion

1981 Chrysler LeBaron Salon

1979 Chrysler LeBaron Medallion

1983 Chrysler LeBaron

1976 Chrysler New Yorker with St. Regis package replaces the 1975 Imperial (below left) as Chrysler's top offering

1975 Imperial – This photograph from the manufacturer's brochure epitomizes the opera window's mystique with the rear seat passenger leaning forward to reveal herself.

1993 Chrysler Imperial – A larger vinyl roof and molding, from the B-pillar back, distinguishes the Imperial from the New Yorker Fifth Avenue (below).

1980 Chrysler New Yorker Fifth Avenue

1993 Chrysler New Yorker Fifth Avenue

1993 Chrysler LeBaron

Starting in 1979, Chrysler stylists adopted a 4-door design metaphor that placed opera windows in the rear door's quarter fixed glass as exemplified by the different roof treatments shown on this page.

1979 Chrysler New Yorker Fifth Avenue

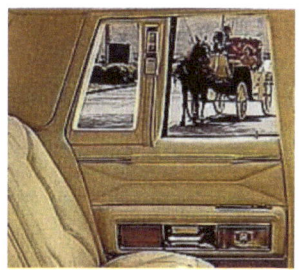
1979 Chrysler New Yorker Fifth Avenue – Inside looking out – Rear seat interior (shown at left) with reading lamp and convenient assist strap.

American Automotive Design Trends: Opera Windows – Fashion over Function

DODGE

1973 Dodge Charger SE

Note on this page the various louvers in the Chargers' windows

1974 Dodge Charger models

1976 Dodge Charger Sport

1975 Dodge Charger SE

1977 Dodge Charger Daytona

American Automotive Design Trends: Opera Windows – Fashion over Function

1981 Dodge Mirada

1979 Dodge Magnum GT

1976 Dodge Aspen Special Edition

1978 Dodge Diplomat Medallion

1976 Dodge Royal Monaco Brougham with forward half-vinyl roof

1979 Dodge Diplomat Salon

1976 Dodge Royal Monaco Brougham with Diplomat Package featuring a padded landau vinyl roof, formal opera windows, framed-in back window, and decorative over-the-top stainless steel band.

1980 Dodge Diplomat S-Type

1975 Dodge Royal Monaco Brougham with full-vinyl roof

1983 Dodge 400

American Automotive Design Trends: Opera Windows – Fashion over Function

FORD

1976 Ford Thunderbird – Cream and Gold Luxury Group

1977 Ford Thunderbird

1977 Ford Thunderbird Town Landau

1978 Ford Thunderbird Diamond Jubilee

1977 Ford Thunderbird Interior Luxury Group

1976 Ford Thunderbird – Cream and Gold Luxury Group – Note Thunderbird insignia on the opera window

1981 Ford Thunderbird Town Landau

1982 Ford Thunderbird Heritage

1976 Ford Elite

1976 Ford Elite – bucket seat option

1977 Ford LTD II Brougham

1975 Ford Elite

1974 Ford Gran Torino

1977 Ford LTD II Brougham

1977 Ford LTD II Brougham

American Automotive Design Trends: Opera Windows – Fashion over Function

1976 Ford LTD Landau

1978 Ford LTD Landau - Brochure refers to this as "Center pillar windows"

1976 Ford Granada Sports Sedan (later called Sports Coupe)

1977 Ford Granada Sports Coupe with opera window louvers

1979 Ford LTD Landau

1979 Ford LTD Luxury Interior Group Option

1987 Ford LTD Crown Victoria – Same basic shape as 1979 with crown molding added

1974 Ford Mustang II Ghia (before opera window added, shown below)

1975 – 1978 Ford Mustang II Ghia (1978 shown)

American Automotive Design Trends: Opera Windows – Fashion over Function

LINCOLN

1976 Lincoln Continental Mark IV – Designer Series

1977 Lincoln Continental Mark V

1977 Lincoln Continental Mark IV – Givenchy with forward half-vinyl roof

1980 Lincoln Continental Mark VI Signature Series

1972 Lincoln Continental Mark IV

1979 Lincoln Continental Mark V – Givenchy interior – Note courtesy / reading lamp integrated into the opera window surround

1980 Lincoln Continental Mark VI

American Automotive Design Trends: Opera Windows – Fashion over Function

1976 Lincoln Continental Town Car

1978 Lincoln Continental (opera window delete)

1977 Lincoln Continental Town Coupé

1980 Lincoln Continental Town Car

1980 Lincoln Continental Town Coupé

1978 Lincoln Continental Town Coupé

1990 Lincoln Town Car

1995 Lincoln Town Car – Using the same basic roofline and opera window dating back to 1980, this design continues until 1997 and is the last opera window offered by any American manufacturer.

American Automotive Design Trends: Opera Windows – Fashion over Function

MERCURY

1976 Mercury Cougar XR-7

1977 Mercury Cougar Brougham

1977 Mercury Cougar Brougham

1977 Mercury Cougar XR-7

1974 Mercury Montego MX Brougham with Custom Trim

1976 Mercury Montego MX

1977 Mercury Cougar XR-7's louvered opera window

American Automotive Design Trends: Opera Windows – Fashion over Function   21

1980 Mercury Cougar XR-7 with Sports Group option – The new design carries forward the louver look from the previous generation, but will be dropped after 1980.

1980 Mercury Cougar XR-7 with Sports Group option

1980 Mercury Cougar XR-7 without the opera window look

1981 Mercury Cougar XR-7 GS with half-vinyl luxury roof

1979 Mercury Grand Marquis Brougham

1983 Mercury Grand Marquis LS – note change in vinyl roof design compared to the 1979 model at left

1977 Mercury Monarch Ghia

1977 Mercury Monarch Ghia rear seat interior

American Automotive Design Trends: Opera Windows – Fashion over Function

OLDSMOBILE

1974 Oldsmobile Cutlass Supreme

(interior)   (exterior)
1974 Oldsmobile Cutlass Salon with Landau roof

1973 Oldsmobile Cutlass without roof treatment

1978 Oldsmobile Cutlass Calais without vinyl roof

1978 Oldsmobile Cutlass Supreme Brougham shown with half-vinyl roof. Labeled as a formal roofline. But, does it qualify for opera window status?

1983 Oldsmobile Cutlass Supreme with Landau Vinyl Rooftop

American Automotive Design Trends: Opera Windows – Fashion over Function

1975 Oldsmobile Ninety-Eight Regency

1975 Oldsmobile Ninety-Eight LS

1977 Oldsmobile Ninety-Eight Regency

1985 Oldsmobile Ninety-Eight Regency Brougham

1977 Oldsmobile Ninety-Eight Regency interior

1984 Cutlass Ciera Holiday Coupe

1975 Oldsmobile Delta 88 Royale

1974 Oldsmobile Delta 88 Royale

1976 Oldsmobile Omega (before landau roof)

1976 Oldsmobile Omega Brougham

1976 Oldsmobile Toronado Brougham (above and right)

1978 Oldsmobile Delta 88 Royale

1980 Oldsmobile Delta 88 Royale

1984 Oldsmobile Toronado Brougham

1984 Oldsmobile Toronado Caliente – Olds adds an opera window look for the Toronado in 1984 and 1985 and calls it the Caliente.

American Automotive Design Trends: Opera Windows – Fashion over Function

PLYMOUTH   *Plymouth*

1977 Plymouth Gran Fury Brougham

1975 Plymouth Gran Fury

1977 Plymouth Fury Sport (without opera window louvers)

1976 Plymouth Fury without opera window

1976 Plymouth Fury Sport with louvered opera window

1977 Plymouth Volaré Premier with Landau roof

1983 Plymouth Reliant Special Edition – fixed rear seat glass bordering on opera window status.

PONTIAC

1976 Pontiac Grand Prix SJ

1978 Pontiac Grand Prix LJ

1984 Pontiac Grand Prix LE

1976 Pontiac Grand LeMans

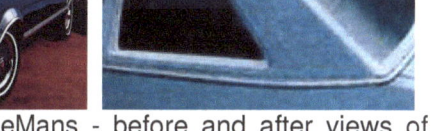

1978 Pontiac Grand LeMans - before and after views of roof treatment that creates the opera window look

1976 Pontiac Ventura SJ

1978 Pontiac Phoenix LJ (formerly Ventura)

American Automotive Design Trends: Opera Windows – Fashion over Function

1976 Pontiac Bonneville with optional Landau roof

1978 Pontiac Bonneville (without Landau roof)

1978 Pontiac Bonneville (with Landau roof)

1984 Pontiac 6000 LE with Landau roof option

1985 Pontiac 6000 (without Landau roof)

1976 Pontiac Catalina Custom – Like its GM siblings with this design, does it or doesn't it have an opera window?

1976 Pontiac Bonneville Brougham

1981 Pontiac Bonneville

1978 Pontiac Sunbird Sport Coupe

Opera Lamps

Recalling the days of some of the earliest carriages and automobiles, manufacturers pay homage to the coach lamp with the introduction of the *Opera Lamp*. Again, Cadillac leads the styling trend in 1971 by introducing the lamps on their 4-door, high-end series as an option (shown below). Opera lamps, like Opera Windows, added period elegance to the design of cars. (My 1980 Lincoln Versailles' B-pillar coach lamp shown at left)

Opera Lamps could be large or small, attached or integrated, and usually reserved for the makes' must opulent trim levels. In the beginning, on 4-door cars they were often found on the C-pillar. Later, designers moved them on some models to the B-pillars. They were illuminated with bulbs or electroluminescence.

1971 Cadillac Fleetwood Sixty Special Brougham

1979 Buick Electra Limited (C-pillar mounted opera lamps)

Opera lamps became a symbol of a well-appointed, luxury model. They were best viewed, illuminated at night. Initially, more lights on a car translated as a design language meaning more luxury. Exterior opera lamps and interior courtesy lights led that trend. Then, more lights equated to more security. Manufacturers introduced options to illuminate the car's interior cabin and exterior key holes. At right is a picture of one of my cars: a 1982 Mercury Cougar XR-7 LS with Luxury Roof option. Here you can see the coach lamp, keyhole light, under-dash courtesy light, door courtesy lamp, and overhead dome light illuminating the car at night.

1984 Buick Electra Park Avenue (B-pillar integrated opera lamps with stainless steel trim)

Even domestically-branded imports could be adorned with opera lamps as shown in this brochure picture below.

1978 Plymouth Sapporo

Some manufacturers cleverly placed opera lamps into moldings for a seamless look or within badges for an even more subtle approach. Below are some examples of opera lamps hidden in badges:

'83 Mercury Cougar LS   '78 Buick Riviera   '79 Ford LTD Landau

Opera lamps were not always present with opera windows and were installed on 2- and 4-door automobiles. Over the next couple of pages, many examples of opera lamps are presented that were not previously included in the prior pages.

American Automotive Design Trends: Opera Windows – Fashion over Function

1979 Buick Riviera

1984 Buick Electra Park Avenue

1977 Cadillac Eldorado

1979 Cadillac Eldorado Biarritz

1974 Cadillac Fleetwood

1979 Cadillac Coupe deVille

1979 Cadillac Fleetwood Brougham

1980 Cadillac Coupe deVille

1985 Cadillac Fleetwood Brougham

1978 Cadillac Seville

1987 Cadillac Fleetwood Brougham d'Elegance

American Automotive Design Trends: Opera Windows – Fashion over Function

1981 Imperial with a Cartier pentastar crystal embedded in the lamp bezel

1977 Chrysler Cordoba with Landau roof

1977 Chrysler Cordoba with halo roof

1977 Chrysler Cordoba with Crown roof and "over-the-top" illuminated lamp band

1982 Chrysler Cordoba

1983 Chrysler New Yorker Fifth Avenue

1979 Chrysler LeBaron

1981 Chrysler LeBaron – Note that the size of the opera lamps seem to double in size compared to 1979.

1979 Chrysler New Yorker

1984 Chrysler New Yorker

American Automotive Design Trends: Opera Windows – Fashion over Function

1979 Ford LTD Landau — Note horizontal shape of opera lamp

1984 Ford LTD Crown Victoria — a more traditional, vertical style

1982 Ford Thunderbird Heritage — Opera lamps are located horizontally under opera window

1983 Ford Thunderbird Heritage — Opera lamps change to a subtle, ornamental look on the C-pillar

1979 Mercury Grand Marquis Colony Park Wagon — Even wagons adopt the opera lamp fashion trend

1977 Lincoln Versailles

1979 Lincoln Versailles — This year, the opera lamps become integrated into a wrap-over, stainless steel roof molding

1975 Lincoln Continental Town Coupé

1975 Lincoln Continental Mark V Cartier edition - Small opera lamp integrated into wrap-over roof molding

1984 Oldsmobile Ninety-Eight Regency

1987 Oldsmobile Ninety-Eight Regency Brougham

1983 Oldsmobile Ciera Brougham

1980 Oldsmobile Cutlass Brougham

1982 Pontiac Grand LeMans

American Automotive Design Trends: Opera Windows – Fashion over Function

INDEX

4
- 400 15

6
- 6000 28

A
- Aspen 15

B
- Barcelona 4
- Biarritz 8, 30
- Bonneville 28
- Brougham 9

C
- Calais 9
- Caprice 10
- Catalina 28
- Century 6
- Charger 14
- Chevelle 11
- Ciera 24, 33
- Colony Park 32
- Concord 4
- Concours 11
- Continental 19, 20
- Cordoba 2, 12, 31
- Cougar 21, 22, 29
- Coupe deVille 9, 30
- Crown Victoria 18, 32
- Cutlass 23, 33

D
- Daytona 14
- Delta 88 25
- Diplomat 15

E
- Eagle 4
- Eldorado 3, 8, 30
- Electra 5, 29, 30
- Elite 17

F
- Fifth Avenue 13, 31
- Fleetwood 9, 29, 30
- Fury 26

G
- Gran Fury 26
- Gran Torino 17
- Granada 18
- Grand LeMans 27, 33
- Grand Marquis 22, 32
- Grand Prix 27

H
- Hornet 4

I
- Impala 10
- Imperial 13, 31

L
- Laguna 11
- LeBaron 12, 31
- LeSabre 5
- LTD 18, 29, 32
- LTD II 17

M
- Magnum 15
- Malibu 11
- Mark IV 3, 19
- Mark V 19, 32
- Mark VI 19
- Matador 4
- Mirada 15
- Monarch 22
- Monte Carlo 11
- Montego 21
- Monza 11
- Mustang II 18

N
- New Yorker 13, 31
- Ninety-Eight 24, 33

O
- Omega 25

P
- Park Avenue 5, 29, 30
- Phoenix 27

R
- Regal 6
- Reliant 26
- Riviera 7, 29, 30
- Royal Monaco 15

S
- Sapporo 29
- Sedan deVille 9
- Seville 30
- Sixty Special 29
- Skylark 6
- Somerset 6
- Sunbird 28

T
- Thunderbird 3, 16, 32
- Toronado 25
- Town Car 3, 20
- Town Coupé 20, 32

V
- Ventura 27
- Versailles 32
- Volaré 26

X
- XR-7 .... 21, 22, 29

www.ingramcontent.com/pod-product-compliance
Lightning Source LLC
Chambersburg PA
CBHW042010150426
43195CB00002B/87